Learning activities for early years

Starting to read and write

Julie Cigman

Illustrations by Alison Dexter

Photographs by John Brennan and Matthew Cannon

Contents

Introduction — 2

Phonics and key words
Making a book — 4
Making cards — 8
Rhyming words — 12
Alphabet fruit salad — 16
Making an information book — 20

Playing with stories
Writing a cumulative story — 24
Becoming familiar with traditional stories — 28
Rewriting a well-known story — 32
Personalising a story — 36
Sequencing a story — 40

Writing for a purpose
Writing in imaginative play — 44
Writing at the post office — 48
Writing at the railway station — 52
Writing recipes and shopping lists — 56
Recording and writing — 60

List of featured books — 64

A & C Black · London

Introduction

Starting to Read and Write offers teachers a range of stimulating ideas for literacy activities that will fulfil the requirements for a comprehensive early years' literacy curriculum, as outlined in the Desirable Outcomes for Children's Learning on Entering Compulsory Education (SCAA 1996).

The early literacy curriculum aims to develop children's understanding:

● that the purpose of reading and writing is communication;

● that reading and writing are used to communicate in different ways and for different purposes;

● of the conventions of print;

● of phonics, rhyme and rhythm in language. It also aims to enable children to become independent in handling and responding to books, and to introduce them to the best of young children's fiction, including British traditional stories and traditional stories from other cultures.

The case studies cover the requirements of the early literacy curriculum, and are designed to:

● motivate children to read and write, by offering stimulating contexts for writing and reading;

● develop children's understanding of the structures of different types of story and non-fiction writing;

● enable children to compose their own writing;

● help them to begin to develop a range of strategies for reading and writing.

Using the case studies

The book is divided into three sections: *Phonics and key words*, *Playing with stories* and *Writing for a purpose*. All of the case studies link in with other curriculum areas and fit in with common nursery themes, such as stories and rhymes, transport, growth and change, food and cooking, and festivals. They are all based on activities which took place in a multi-cultural city nursery school, involving three- and four-year-old children from a wide range of social backgrounds, some of whom had English as a second language.

Phonics and key words

These case studies introduce children to the decoding and encoding skills needed for early reading and writing. They also introduce children to a small sight vocabulary, in a context. The activities help them to develop and extend their understanding of letter/sound correspondence, onset and rime.

Playing with stories

The case studies in this section are designed to help children to understand how stories work, to see themselves as authors and to develop an awareness of audience. They see adults behaving as writers and act as writers themselves. Learning about the structure of stories helps children to write their own stories.

The activities introduce children to a range of strategies for reading: onset, rime, using context, using syntactical clues, and prediction. In addition they will learn about:

● story language – once upon a time .... long, long ago .... and they got back in time for tea;

● patterns and rhythm of language;

● predicting the outcome of a story;

● sequencing events of a story;

● telling a story from pictures as well as the text.

Writing for a purpose

These case studies are designed to develop children's understanding that writing is a means of expression and communication. The children are given contexts for writing for different reasons and for reading different types of writing.

The case studies give children the opportunity to practise the secretarial skills of writing:

● letter formation;

● writing in straight lines, from the top to the bottom of the page and from left to right.

They also encourage the compositional skills of writing by introducing children to the conventions of different kinds of writing:

● messages;

● recipes, menus and shopping lists;

● letters and cards;

● signs and labels;

● recording information.

Differentiation

The case studies support nursery staff in providing literacy activities that are relevant to the stages of development and conceptual understanding of individual children. Examples are given of ways in which different children might respond to activities, and suggestions are made for suitable adult intervention, which will help to support and extend their learning.

Extension activities

Each of the case studies has ideas for extension activities, suitable for children with a range of special needs, including bilingual children, children with physical disabilities and children who are already beginning to read and write independently.

The case studies offer structured activities, but it is also suggested that children should have plenty of opportunities to read and write in their play. As with other areas of learning, children develop literacy skills and understanding best when their learning is self-motivated and when they have plenty of time to practice, with adult support.

Working with parents

Children learn about reading and writing well before they start formal learning at school. They see people reading and writing at home; they see print all around them; they look at books and hear stories on television and tapes. This helps them to understand the purpose and value of literacy in the day-to-day context of home and the family.

Parents are a valuable resource. Schools can encourage and support them by talking about how they have helped, and can carry on helping their children.

Making a book

Intended learning

For the children to develop a range of strategies for reading; to retell a story; to recognise some letter shapes and write and read their name; to work as part of a group – speaking and listening.

Introduction

This is a group-time activity, which gives children a simple structure to help them to create their own stories. Read together a simple traditional story that has repeated phrases that the children can remember and so join in. An adult can scribe the children's version of the story, talking about sounds, words and phrases as she writes. The children can be encouraged to write their names and some keywords.

Key vocabulary

pop, pull, turnip;
the children's own names

The activity

You will need:

A copy of *The Enormous Turnip* by Nicola Baxter (Ladybird), some root vegetables and labels for them, a box filled with some brown tissue paper, a large blank zigzag book (made from large white paper) and some felt-tipped pens.

● Read the story of *The Enormous Turnip* and make sure that the children are familiar with the pattern of the language.

● Look at a turnip and some other root vegetables, then write the different names on the labels and make a display of them in the classroom. Talk about how plants and vegetables grow.

● The children could help an adult to retell the story with storyboard pictures. This can take place over several group sessions.

● Hide a turnip in a box filled with brown tissue paper. Ask the children to guess what is hidden and then look to see if they are right. Lift the turnip out to see how heavy it is, then tell the story again, encouraging them to join in.

● Let one child role-play 'planting' the turnip and then trying to pull it out of the 'ground'. This child then chooses another to help her, and he chooses another, and so on until there is one child left. Encourage them to predict at each stage whether they will be able to pull the turnip out. They will love the domino effect as 'they pull the turnip out of the ground – with a POP!'

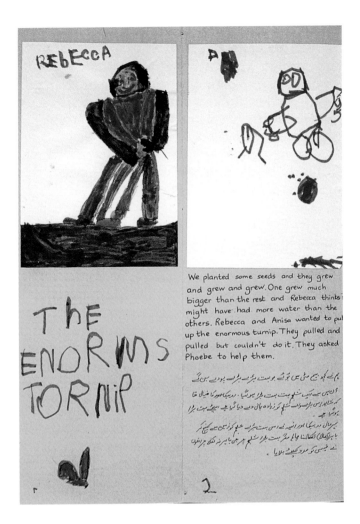

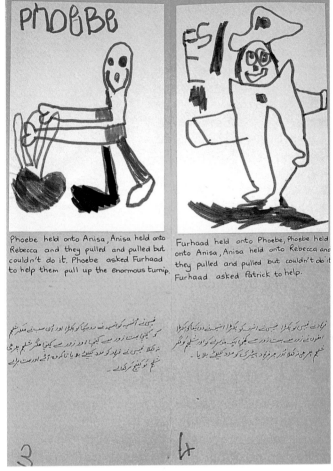

• Using the blank zigzag book, ask a child to draw an enormous turnip and him/herself trying to pull it out of the ground. Ask the others to remember who had come to help next, and let them draw themselves in turn, holding on to the child in front. On the last page, they could draw a large pot of turnip soup!

• The children's version of the story could be written for them under their pictures and they could write their names.

The children's words were scribed by the teacher in English and translated into Urdu. The story was read back to the children in English and Urdu.

• Once children have become familiar with the story language, they will be able to tell the story, using the pictures and their names to help them sequence the events. Some children might notice that every time the story is read, the words are the same, but when they tell the story, they sometimes use different words.

• Children can be encouraged to talk about detail in the pictures and elements of the story which aren't in the pictures.

Assessment

● Can the children retell the traditional version of the story and the version that they acted out? Can they follow their own version of the story in the zigzag book?

● Do the children recognise themselves as authors of the zigzag book? Can they write their names? Can they find their names in the book?

● Do the children use a range of strategies when they retell the story from the zigzag book they helped write? Do they use picture clues, memory of repeated phrases and word recognition (their own names)?

Evidence of children's learning

The structure of the zigzag book helped the children to see that we read from left to right. Many of them were able to write and read their names. Some of them wrote 'pull' and lot of them wrote 'pop', as the turnip came out of the ground. Most of them were able to join in when the story was retold.

Differentiating the activity

For children who have problems following sequences, make an obstacle course or a circuit in the garden. Talk about the sequence as they follow it: "Over the frame, through the tunnel...."

Similarly, make and follow patterns using mosaics, pegboards and printing.

Further experience of cumulative stories will also help those children to follow the sequence.

Having access to blank books is useful for all children. Those who are simply mark-making will have the experience of writing, using appropriate tools and making marks from left to right. Children with more advanced reading and writing skills will enjoy having a smaller version of the blank zigzag book, choosing a different story and drawing and writing about it in their own book.

This is me. I like playing on the computer.

Extension activities

● If it is the right time of year, you could sow some root vegetables, such as radishes and carrots, or visit an allotment to see some growing.

● The children could make their own zigzag books, using other traditional stories or writing their own.

● Make zigzag books with pictures relating to children's interests: things they see on the way to nursery; things they did as a baby, a toddler, as a four year old...

● Make some vegetable soup, using turnips and other vegetables. Write the recipe as another sequencing activity.

● Print with vegetables. Some children will be able to follow a repeat pattern.

● Read and act out other cumulative stories.

A computer. I like using the computer. My brother has a computer.
AATIKAH

Working with parents

● Visit an allotment or vegetable garden of willing parents!

● Encourage parents to read the children's story with their child when they come to the nursery, and to look at the display of vegetables. They could help the children to match the vegetables with their labels.

● Encourage parents from other cultures to share their traditional stories. Any particularly good stories could be taped and a children's book or storyboard pictures made to go with the tape.

Other stories to use

Who Sank the Boat?
by Pamela Allen (Puffin)

The story of a group of animals that climb into a boat one at a time. The boat is seen to sink lower into the water each time an animal climbs in. Will the cow sink the boat? Or the pig? This is another story that could be acted out. It would work well with storyboard pictures, as the boat could be moved lower in the water and the animals tipped out.

The Gingerbread Man
retold by Brenda Parkes and Judith Smith (Mimosa Publications)

The Runaway Chappatti
by Ruth Creek (E J Arnold)

These are two versions of a similar story, with more and more characters joining in the chase. *The Gingerbread Man* is a big book which is useful for group work.

Making cards

Intended learning

For the children to understand that print carries a message and that, in English, print goes from left to right and top to bottom of the page; to understand the conventions of greetings cards, that the picture is usually on the front and the writing inside; to learn to recognise and write some letter shapes and learn the sounds that some letters make; to learn the key words for card making, including writing their own name and beginning to memorise their own address.

Introduction

This activity involves making greetings cards for Mother's Day, but it could be adapted for any other festival. Some festivals will have more relevance to some children than others. Cards made for the Muslim festival of Eid-ul-fitr (which marks the end of Ramadan) open from left to right and have writing in Arabic from right to left. These offer an interesting talking point and can be compared with cards for other festivals.

Key vocabulary

address, back, dear, envelope, front, Happy Mother's Day, inside, love from, stamps, to,

x x x x x

The activity

You will need:

pieces of card of different colours and sizes, drawing materials, collage materials such as sequins, coloured feathers, shiny paper, glitter, coloured pasta and rice, large envelopes and stamps.

● Talk about the different occasions when we send cards to other people. Some of the children could bring in cards from home. Discuss what the cards looked like, the types of pictures, the use of colour and the sorts of words that are used. Making cards for different festivals helps children to value other cultures, and helps minority cultures to feel valued.

● Provide collage materials, with cards of different sizes and colours and let the children choose their own collage materials and design the card themselves. This is a good opportunity to discuss the form of a card, and to make sure that they open it and hold it the right way.

● Encourage them to write something inside the card. If the children are mark-making, encourage them to give the marks meaning by asking them what they have written. Alternatively, ask them what they want to say and either scribe the message or help them to work out the sounds. Let them write their name in the card and draw kisses.

● Provide envelopes and help them to write the name of the person (Mummy) and the address. Let them stick a stamp on their own envelope and, if possible, go out in groups to post the cards. Posting the card and seeing it arrive helps children to understand why it is important for each house to have a different address and why the postman and woman have to be able to read.

The children learned about the conventions of cards by talking to an adult as they created their own cards.

Assessment

● Do the children understand which is the front and which is the back of the card, and which is the inside?

● Do they understand the concept of sending a written message? Can they say what they would like to write? Can they write a message?

● Can they write their own names? Can they recognise and name some letter shapes? Do they know some letter sounds?

● Do they know their parents' names, or do they just want to write 'Mummy' on the envelope? Do they know their address? Can they write the number of their house or flat? Do they know how a letter gets from one place to another and can they explain the process?

Evidence of the children's learning

Some children stuck materials randomly onto the card; others created some patterns. Some wanted to stick things inside the card and this was used as a discussion point – the picture is usually on the front of the card and the message is written on the inside. However, children were allowed to stick things inside if they felt strongly, as they were encouraged to feel that they were creating the card them-selves, not following someone else's design.

Some children wrote confidently – mark-making, writing recognisable words – Mummy, love, their own name. Other children needed a lot of encouragement to verbalise a message or to write something in the card.

Differentiating the activity

For children who can't verbalise a message, provide some key words. This will give them a structure to work to.

Some children will make marks in the card and some will write random letters. If they can 'talk their message', this can be scribed for them. The connection between the letter shapes and the sounds can be talked about as an adult writes for them.

Those who have some understanding of letter-sound correspondence can be helped to write a message themselves, using independent spelling. For those who can write their name, the connection between the letters and sounds in their name and other words can be pointed out.

Children who are beginning to write independently can be shown some key words: To, Dear, love from. All children can be shown how to draw kisses.

Using collage materials gives children a chance to work with different textures and colours, and encourages the development of fine motor skills.

Extension activities

● Set up a post office role-play area with cards, envelopes, paper, pretend stamps and different writing materials. This allows children at all stages of early literacy development to experiment with mark-making and writing. It also helps them to learn about reasons for writing.

- Send messages – at group time – from one group of children to another; from one member of staff to another. Talk to the children about what the message says, and ask them to deliver the message.

- The children could make cards for other festivals.

- Use card and envelopes to make cards for friends and family.

Different festivals provide opportunities for making different kinds of cards.

Working with parents

- Explain the purpose of this activity to parents, and ask for their support – in providing a stamp, if possible; in talking to their child about how they made the card and how the card arrived at their house.

- Ask the parents to help their children to learn their own addresses.

- Ask parents from other cultures to bring in examples of greetings cards for their own festivals.

Other books to read

These are all books about writing and sending letters and messages.

The Jolly Postman
by Janet and Alan Ahlberg (Heinemann)

The Jolly Postman has letters, postcards and invitations which relate to many of the traditional stories that children know well. This book will stimulate card- and letter-writing based on these stories or on the children's own experiences.

Wish You Were Here
by Martina Selway (Red Fox)

Wish You Were Here tells the story of a child's visit to a camp through writing letters to different members of her family.

Dear Zoo
by Rod Campbell (Puffin)

A child who is looking for an animal as a pet writes a letter to the zoo.

Rhyming words

Intended learning

For the children to recognise and make up rhyming words; to develop listening skills; to extend their vocabulary; to write their names.

Introduction

For this activity, we chose *The Fish Who Could Wish* by John Bush and Korky Paul, a book that uses rhyming language to tell a simple story. After we had read it to the children we encouraged them to think up their own simple rhyming sentences. They were asked to listen carefully and this helped them to become more accurate in their use and understanding of rhyming words. A developing understanding of sounds and patterns in language gives young children a good foundation from which they can tackle the decoding and encoding skills of reading and writing.

Key vocabulary

fish, wish, the children's own names and other words that rhyme with their names

The activity

You will need:

The Fish Who Could Wish by John Bush and Korky Paul (OUP); paper for scribing the children's words and for their drawings; coloured pencils and felt-tipped tips.

● Read the story of *The Fish Who Could Wish* with the children.

● Play rhyming games with the children's names, finding nonsense or real words that rhyme – Poppy the Floppy, Marley the Farley, Ijaz the Pijaz.

● Read other stories that are written in rhyme, letting the children try to guess words at the end of the line, using the rhyme and context to help them, for example *My Cat Likes to Hide in Boxes* by Eve Sutton, *Pointy-hatted Princesses* by Nick Sharratt and *Caveman Dave* by Nick Sharratt.

● Ask a group of children to come and work together. They will need to have an understanding of rhyme in songs, stories and poems. Encourage them to play around with rhyming words and make sure they are familiar with the story *The Fish Who Could Wish*. Talk about the kinds of things they might wish for.

● To start the children off, play with rhyming words based on the story. For example, Trish wished for a fish, June wished to go to the moon and so on. They will get the idea quickly and respond to questions such as 'What would Clare wish for?' 'Clare would wish for a chair ...a bear ...a fair ...a pear...'

The display encouraged the children to read back the sentences that they had made up.

● This is an opportunity to introduce new vocabulary. For example, it could be suggested that Clare might wish for a hare.

● Finally, ask the children what they would really wish for. Let them write their name and an adult can scribe their rhyming sentences and their real wishes. They could illustrate these and their drawings and scribed words could be put up on a display. Encourage them to remember and 'read' the sentence that they have written.

Assessment

● Can the children hear when words rhyme?

● Can they find a rhyme for simple words? Can they find a rhyme for their name?

● Can they find pairs of rhyming words that together have meaning, such as fat cat?

● Do they have fun playing with the sounds of words and making nonsense rhymes?

● Can they recognise when a word nearly rhymes, but isn't an exact rhyme?

● Can they find appropriate adjectives to describe their rhyming nouns?

● Can they write their name?

Evidence of children's learning

The children all found words to rhyme with their names. Some of the words were nonsense, but rhymed; some made sense and nearly rhymed (Georgia wished for a recorder); and some made sense and rhymed! When they had found an appropriate noun that rhymed with their name, they were encouraged to think of an adjective, to help extend their vocabulary.

Clare wished for a cuddly bear
(a bunny really!)
Ben wished for ten men (a castle really!)
Esme wished for a magic key (a castle really!)
Meg wished for a peg (a rabbit and a
Dalmatian called Pongo really!)
Ben wished for a pen (a polar bear really!)
Georgia wished for a recorder (a rabbit really!)

Differentiating the activity

Children will need to hear lots of rhyming stories, poems and songs before they can produce their own rhymes. Some will have had a lot of experience at home, others will need to be introduced to rhyming patterns at nursery school.

Some children might need help with writing unfamiliar letters in their name. It might be appropriate to draw their attention to upper and lower case letters, for example on the computer keyboard. It might be useful to talk about letter-sound correspondence.

Listening to rhymes and songs helps children develop phonological awareness, for when they start to read. Action rhymes and songs encourage them to join in before they have the active language skills, and some may start to join in with a chorus, repeated words, or simply the rise and fall of the tune.

Clapping games, where they listen to and copy a rhythm, will help to develop concentration and listening skills.

Some children will be able to look at rhyming words with simple letter blends (oo and ee).

Some children could make little books, with pictures of rhyming pairs of words.

Extension activities

● Make up verses for songs using rhyming words –
When I was one, I'd just begun...
When I was two, I grew and grew...

Who's that knocking at my door?
'It's not I,' said the rat, 'It's not I,' said the cat...
'It's not I' said the bee, 'It's not I' said the tree...

● Read *Don't Put Your Finger in the Jelly, Nelly* by Nick Sharratt. Make a book using children's names: Don't put your finger on the spike, Mike. Don't put your finger on the brick, Nick.

● Give the children a word, then act out or draw another word that rhymes with it. See if they guess the rhyming word. For example, give them the word 'plum' and then wave your thumb around; say 'flag' and then draw a zigzag or put things in a bag.

Working with parents

● Encourage parents to sing songs and rhymes with children at home, and to read stories written in rhyme.

● Ask them to tell the children their own names and, if possible, to find words that rhyme with them. They could write these down for the children to bring in to school.

● Write out the words of some rhymes or rhyming songs on the computer and make copies for parents to use with children at home. The children could help to illustrate them.

Other books to read

Cops and Robbers
by Janet and Alan Ahlberg (Fontana Picture Lions)

Where's My Teddy?
by Jez Alborough (Walker Books)

This Is the Bear
by Sarah Hayes and Helen Craig (Walker Books)

These three books all have a strong rhythm as well as rhyming words which help to develop phonic awareness. Children can be encouraged to listen to the rhyme and rhythm and predict rhyming words at the end of a line ('With a sudden leap, he bounded free... And handcuffed Horace to a nearby... [tree].')

Left: Writing spells can encourage children to think about rhyme and rhythmic patterns of language.

Alphabet fruit salad

Intended learning

For the children to learn the names and sounds of some of the letters of the alphabet; to learn to recognise the initial sound of a word; to know the sound that different letters make (letter/sound correspondence).

Introduction

This activity helps children to understand onset – a skill essential for early reading and independent writing. This is the ability to recognise the initial sound of a word, and the understanding that there is a letter that corresponds to that sound.

Key vocabulary

bowl, chop, fruit salad, stir, names of the different kinds of fruit – apples, apricots, bananas, grapes, kiwi fruit, lemon, melon, mango, nectarines, oranges, pears, peaches, plums, star fruit, strawberries

The activity

You will need:

Ingredients for a fruit salad – a range of common and exotic fruits; knives, chopping boards, and a large bowl; pictures of different kinds of fruit; card, plastic or vinyl letter shapes; a large piece of paper and some thick felt-tipped pens.

● Teach the children the rhyme 'Chop, chop, chop, chop'... letting them choose any ingredients.

Chop, chop, chop, chop
Chop off the bottom and chop off the top,
All the rest goes into the pot,
Chop, chop, chop, chop.

Stir the fruit salad, stir the fruit salad.
Have a little taste...
What this fruit salad needs is...
Something beginning with mmm... melon!

● Set up a table with small chopping boards, knives and a large bowl. Encourage the children to come and choose some fruit to chop and add to the bowl. While this is happening, the other children could play an 'I spy...' game:

'I spy with my little eye something beginning with sssssssss...'
'Strawberries! – "Who wants to chop some strawberries?"'

● Make a display of different kinds of fruit and talk about their names. Then say the 'Chop, chop' rhyme.

● Let the children choose things to put into a pretend fruit salad beginning with a particular sound and find or draw the letter sound to match.

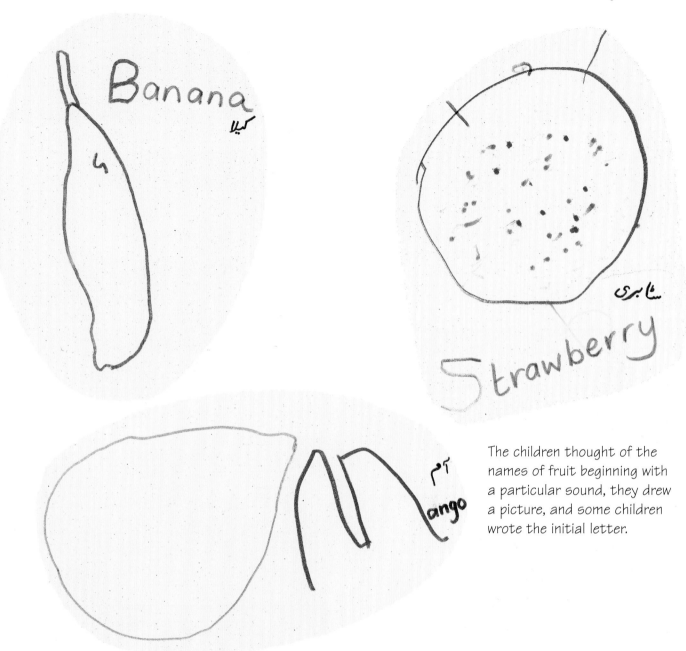

Banana کیلا

Strawberry سٹابری

ango آم

The children thought of the names of fruit beginning with a particular sound, they drew a picture, and some children wrote the initial letter.

● Draw a big bowl in the middle of a large piece of paper. Look at the fruit in the display, and talk about the initial sound of each fruit. Some children could write the initial letters of some fruit around the bowl and an adult write the rest of the word until the names of all of the fruit are on the paper.

● Go back to the picture on the following day and remind the children of the names of the fruit and the initial sound of each word. Let them draw pictures of the fruit in the bowl, with arrows connecting the picture with the writing.

Evidence of children's learning

Some children were very quick and could think of fruit beginning with the correct sound. Others needed time to look at the fruit on display. Still others watched and listened. We linked the initial sounds of the names of the fruit with the initial sounds of the children's names: 'Mmmm for melon, Mmmm for Minnie!'

Assessment

● Can the children isolate and say the sound at the beginning of a word? They are likely to do this with differing degrees of accuracy: a child might say grapes begins with 'g...', 'grr...', or 'gray...'

● Can they think of other words that have the same initial sound?

● Can the children recognise the letter that makes the same sound as the initial sound of a word?

● Can the children recognise some letters of the alphabet, identifying them by name or sound (either upper or lower case)? Can they write some recognisable letter shapes? Can they name the letters that they have written correctly?

Differentiating the activity

Some children will know the names, but not the sounds of letters. The following game helps to develop listening skills and concentration.

Ask the children to sit in a circle with one child in the middle. Place several instruments in the middle of the circle, for example bells, a drum, a tambourine, and a shaker. (Choose instruments that make distinctive sounds). To the tune of 'Oats and Beans and Barley Grow...', the children sing:

Mrs (or Mr) Bear lives in a cave.
Mrs Bear lives in a cave.
Now who will dare, now who will dare
To steal a sound from Mrs Bear?

The child in the middle closes her eyes and a child is chosen to creep into the circle and play an instrument. The child in the middle has to listen hard, and guess which instrument has been played.

Another musical game is follow the leader. Someone makes a sound with an instrument, or by clapping or singing and everyone else has to make the same sound.

Extension activities

● Some children could make shopping lists and small books with pictures of things beginning with the same letter as their name.

● Sing or chant:

Mr Bear, Mr Bear, won't you come to tea,
Come next Monday at half past three
Cakes and biscuits there will be
And there will be lots for you and me!

The children can choose things for tea which begin with different sounds.

● Read *The Very Hungry Caterpillar* by Eric Carle, and draw pictures of food that the caterpillar ate beginning with different sounds.

● Play a game where you go shopping and can only buy things beginning with a particular sound: milk, melons, maps, a monkey, a Metro, mittens... The children might be able to think of some sensible and some not so sensible suggestions!

Working with parents

● Talk to parents about the value of making shopping lists with their children and talking about the sounds of the words as they write them.

● Suggest that parents play 'I spy' when they are out in the car, on a bus or walking home. Stress that the game should be fun for children and it doesn't matter if they make mistakes.

Left: Listening to and playing rhythm patterns with musical instruments helps children to become familiar with the rhythmic patterns of spoken language.

Other books to read

The Very Hungry Caterpillar
by Eric Carle (Puffin)

Handa's Surprise
by Eileen Browne (Walker Books)

Both of these books can be used to encourage children to think about the initial sounds of different types of fruit or other food. *The Very Hungry Caterpillar* eats his way through a wide range of fruits and, in *Handa's Suprise*, Handa sets out with a basket of fruit on her head. The fruit disappears piece by piece, taken by different culprits, but Handa manages to arrive at her friend's house with a basket of different fruit, much to her surprise.

ABC Dinosaurs
by Jan Pienkowski (Heinemann)

This will appeal to may dinosaur-obsessed children. They can look at the initial letters and have fun listening to the sounds of the dinosaurs' names.

A Is for Africa
by Ifeoma Onyefulu (Frances Lincoln)

This books shows children a different way of life in Africa, through an alphabet book.

ABC Zoo
by Rod Campbell (Puffin)

This is a simple, straightforward alphabet book with some flaps.

Making an information book

Intended learning

For the children to use initial sounds to identify words; to write and read their own names; to match writing and pictures – recognising words in context; to follow instructions in a sequence.

Introduction

This activity gives children a purpose for writing, providing an opportunity to talk about letter shapes and sounds, and encouraging them to try and read words in context. It encourages them to work as a group, with the teacher providing a model of a writer.

Key vocabulary

compost, grow; plants, pots, seeds; the children's own names; the names of seeds – runner beans, peas, cornflowers, corn, lettuce; water

The activity

You will need:

Small plant pots (or yoghurt pots with holes in the bottom) – at least one for each child; a large bag of multi-purpose potting compost; a variety of different size seeds (runner beans, peas, sweet peas, nasturtiums, tomatoes, lettuces, cornflowers); a tray to display the pots on, a watering can, sticky labels, sequencing cards; a camera and film; sheets of white drawing paper and pencils; a home-made book or large photograph album in which to record the work.

● Introduce the activity by telling the story of Jack and the Beanstalk. There is a good version by Tony Ross (Picture Ladybird). Talk about the five magic beans which the old man gave to Jack, and how they grew into a gigantic beanstalk.

● Put out plant pots, compost and seeds and let the children choose seeds to plant.

Talk about the sequence of planting and caring for seeds. Observe the children's ability to listen carefully, follow instructions and follow the sequence:

　　fill a plant pot with compost
　　soak the compost in water
　　plant the seed in the compost
　　cover the seed with compost
　　water the seeds regularly.

● When the children have planted their seeds, let them write their names and the names of their seeds on labels. Alternatively, they can watch as an adult writes for them. Let them stick the labels on their pots.

The children used the photographs and drawings to help them read the book with an adult.

● Take photographs while the children are planting the seeds. These can be used as sequencing cards or made into a book. The children's drawings of the seedlings and plants can be added to make a record of the activity – a book with a beginning, an end and a sequence of events in between. An adult can scribe their words, helping them to understand that written words carry meaning. They should write their names as authors of the book.

● Children can talk about the people in the photographs and what they are doing, which helps them to talk through the sequence of the activity. They can look at the writing with an adult, and match the text to the pictures. This helps them to develop an understanding that print carries meaning.

Assessment

● Are the children willing to have a go at writing their name? Can they write some of the letters correctly? Do they use upper and lower case letters appropriately? Can they write their name correctly?

● Are the children willing to have a go at writing the name of the seeds on a label? Can they recognise the name of the seeds and their own name on the labels on their plant pot? Do they use pictures to help them to read labels or captions in the seed book? Do they use the initial sound of a word to help them to read the labels or captions in the seed book?

● Can children follow instructions in a sequence? Can they tell an adult what the sequence of actions should be?

● Do they hold the book the right way up and turn the pages from front to back? Can they match text and pictures? Can they recognise any words that they, or other children or adults, have written?

Evidence of children's learning

The children used the photographs to 'read' the words, helping them to understand the relationship between pictures and text. Following the sequence helped them to understand that we read print from left to right. Writing the book helped to develop their vocabulary and encouraged them to form clear sentences. They enjoyed reading a book that they had helped to write. This encouraged them to behave like readers: handling books, turning the pages, talking a story.

Differentiating the activity

Some children found sequencing cards useful. These were made by drawing simple pictures relating to the sequence of the activity.

Some children will show confidence as writers but will not make any recognisable letter shapes. Teachers can write their name by their writing, talking about the letter sounds.

Others will write some of the letters in their name correctly, but might reverse some letters, or leave some out. Missing or incorrect letters can be pointed out at an appropriate time, without undermining their confidence.

Some children will use upper and lower case letters interchangeably, as they see both all around them. Their attention can be drawn to differences and similarities in print around the nursery, such as upper case on the computer keyboard and lower case on the screen, but they do not need to be corrected at this stage.

Reading the name of seeds from a seed packet helps them to recognise words in a context, and to use the initial sound and pictures to identify a word. Some children can attempt independent spelling once they have an understanding of letter–sound correspondence. Adults can provide a model of a writer for children, talking about letter sounds and shapes in a context.

Reading the book with an adult will help children to learn to handle the book correctly and talk about the words and pictures.

Right: Each of the children wrote their name on to a label so they knew which pot was theirs as they watched the progress of the seeds they'd planted.

Extension activities

● Set up a matching activity – matching seeds with seed packets, and written labels with seeds and pictures.

● Draw faces on egg shells and plant cress or grass seed to make the hair. Take photos 'before' and 'after'. Make up names for the egg faces and write labels with their names on.

● Cut open apples, oranges, pears and other fruit and look at the seeds inside. Draw pictures and write the names of fruits that have seeds.

● Make prints with fruit and vegetables on paper and material. Use the pictures and material to make a display, labelling different kinds of fruit and vegetables, including some exotic kinds.

Working with parents

● The children could take their seedlings home to plant out, if they have a garden.

● Encourage the children to read the book that they have made with their parents.

● Encourage the children to talk to their parents about their work on displays.

● The children might like to make books at home with their parents and bring them to show the teachers.

Other books to use

Jaspar's Beanstalk
by Nick Butterworth and Mick Inkpen (Hodder Children's Books)

Jaspar's Beanstalk follows the same sequence that the children follow when they sow their seeds, so it helps to reinforce this pattern. It also follows the sequence of the days of the week. Children who know the order of the days of the week can be encouraged to use the initial letter of the word to 'read' it – "On T....Tuesday", "On W....Wednesday" and so on.

Titch
by Pat Hutchins (Picture Puffin)

In *Titch*, a small boy sows a seed with a surprise result. The story has very clear picture clues which help children to join in and predict words as they listen to the story.

The Tiny Seed
by Eric Carle (Puffin)

Mouse Finds a Seed
by Nicola Moon, illustrated by Anthony Morris (Pavilion)

The Tiny Seed and *Mouse Finds a Seed* both use stories to explain the conditions that seeds need in order to grow.

Writing a cumulative story

Intended learning

For the children to develop speaking and listening skills; to learn about the language and structure of a story; to sequence events and retell a story; to read and write signs and labels; to extend vocabulary.

Introduction

The Elephant and the Bad Baby by Elfrida Vipont and Raymond Briggs is just one of many stories that lend themselves to being 'played around with'. The elephant takes the bad baby for a ride and offers different treats along the way, such as a lollipop, an apple and a bag of crisps. The baby is 'bad' because he never says 'please' when these things are offered.

Everytime the elephant takes something for the bad baby, they are chased by the shop keeper or stall holder and the line of people chasing them gets longer and longer. The story culminates in them all going home and eating pancakes.

The simple structure of the story helps children to become story tellers. In this activity, a small group of children were asked to focus on, and change, just one element of the story. Between them, they created a new story with the same structure, helping them to understand how stories work.

Key vocabulary

bad baby, elephant, please
rumpeta, rumpeta, rumpeta
all down the road ... the elephant
took a ... for himself and a ...
for the bad baby with ... running
after

The activity

You will need:
A copy of *The Elephant and the Bad Baby* by Elfrida Vipont and Raymond Briggs, some pieces of coloured paper or card for labels, felt-tipped pens, paper on which to scribe the children's story.

● Read the story to help the children become familiar with the pattern and the repeated phrases.

● Then retell the story, explaining to the children that you need their help, as you don't know where the elephant and the bad baby are going next. As the story develops, each child can suggest a place for the elephant and the bad baby to visit. These ideas can be written down as a 'sign' on a piece of coloured card, by the child alone, by the child with help or by the teacher. This is an opportunity to talk about letter/sound correspondence. Attention can be drawn to the initial letter of a word as a clue. Now let children tell what the elephant would take at each place he visited.

● The story should be retold, this time using the children's suggestion cards as prompts. Encourage them to recognise their own cards and to join in with repeated phrases.
Teacher: 'Then they came to a...'
Everyone: '...sweet shop!'

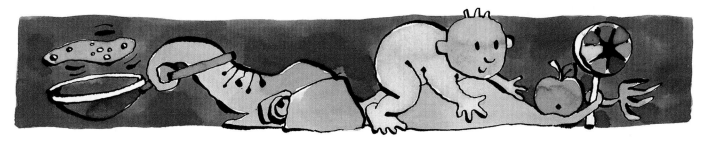

The children read their own labels. They read the story with their parents or other adults in the nursery.

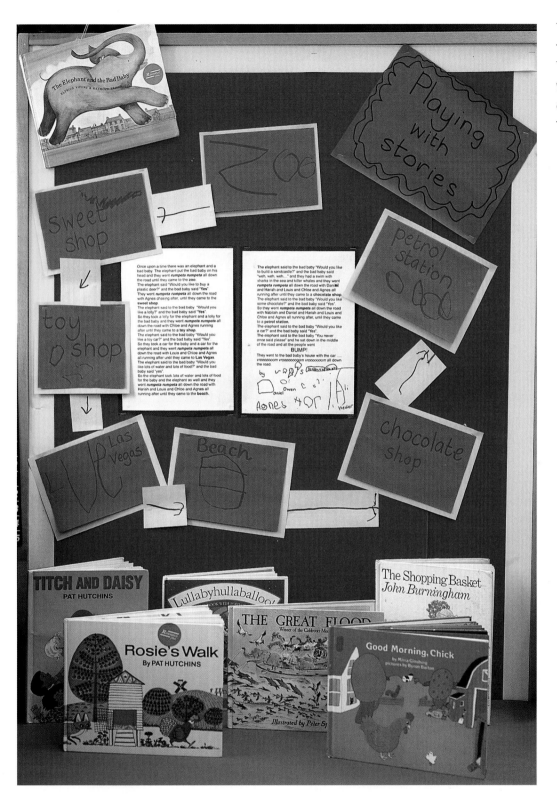

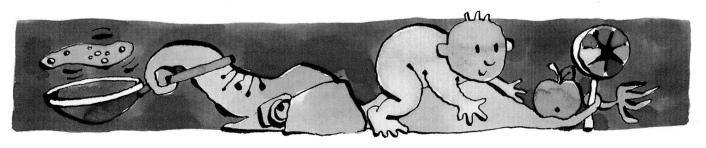

Assessment

● Can the children listen well to the story and join in with the repeated phrases?

● Can they follow the sequence of the story?

● Can they contribute a suggestion for a place for the elephant and the bad baby to go to, and something for the elephant to take?

● Can they have a go at writing their suggestion on a piece of card?

● Can they recognise their own signs, and those of others?

● Can the children retell the story in their own words, using the scribed story as a prompt?

Evidence of the children's learning

The children were able to join in with repeated phrases:

'Then they came to a ...'
'and the elephant took a ... for himself
and a ... for the bad baby ...'
'and they went rumpeta, rumpeta, rumpeta all down the road with (child's name added) running after.'

At a second session, they were able to tell the story, while the teacher scribed their words. Some children had a go at writing their own signs.

Differentiating the activity

Some children will join in immediately, others will develop confidence as they become more familiar with the story. Children may need to listen a lot before they join in. At this point, they are developing their story language. Children who are unwilling to speak might respond to a suggestion from the teacher with a nod. The teacher may be able to use their special interests to encourage them to respond.

Some children might make marks on paper: the teacher can encourage them, then scribe the words for the child, while talking about the letters and sounds. Others might write the initial sound of a word: the teacher can then add the rest of the word, talking about the letters and sounds. Others might write the sign with a mixture of emergent and conventional spellings. Children who are beginning to write independently can be encouraged to write signs and labels for other purposes in the nursery. If a child is unwilling to write anything, the teacher can scribe his or her words, talking to the child as she writes.

Bilingual children may need the support of a mother tongue teacher if this is possible. Children who don't speak English can be encouraged to talk in their first language. They might need a period of silence before they start to speak in English.

The repetition of words and phrases is useful for children with limited spoken language.

Involving children actively in story telling helps develop their concentration, by engaging their interest. It might help extend the time that children can sit still and listen.

Early story writing. It says 'Once upon a time lived the three bears, baby bear, mummy'.

Extension activities

● Like the elephant and the bad baby, the children could help to mix pancake batter and have some pancakes. This is an opportunity for looking at print on labels and packets, and for writing a recipe.

● A shop selling the items that were featured in the story could be set up as a role play area, with signs and labels for the different items.

● Use scrap card to make signs, labels and recipes.

Working with parents

● Invite a parent in to help make the pancakes at group time.

● This story can be told on Shrove Tuesday. Invite parents from different ethnic backgrounds to come in and share stories from their festivals at appropriate times.

● Encourage children to share their book about the elephant and the bad baby with their parents at the beginning of the nursery session.

Other books to read

The Doorbell Rang
by Pat Hutchins (Puffin)

This book tells the story of two children sitting down to share a big plate of biscuits. The doorbell keeps ringing and more and more children come and join them around the kitchen table – and so their share of biscuits becomes smaller and smaller.

So Much
by Trish Cooke, illustrated by Helen Oxenbury (Walker Books)

Different people come to visit Mum and the baby. Each time someone comes in, they come and play with the baby, who they love SO MUCH. The language develops with repeated phrases, a strong rhythm and takes pleasure in the sounds of words. Children will be able to join in with the intonation and rhythm of the language, and will quickly predict what is going to happen.

Ten In the Bed
by Penny Dale (Walker Books)

This is an illustrated version of the song, with plenty of repetition. Children can act out the story or just join in with actions for 'roll over'.

Becoming familiar with traditional stories

Intended learning

For the children to have experience in handling books and become familiar with traditional stories; to understand the difference between print and pictures; to develop skills in writing for a reason – labels, recipes, lists; to learn to write their own names.

Introduction

Reading a book again and again helps children to become familiar with the story, while still having time to stop and talk about detail in the pictures. Reading a story straight through helps them to learn that story language is different from conversation. The pictures help to give clues as to what is going to happen next and help children when they start to read independently.

Stories are a good starting point from which children can be encouraged to talk, draw pictures and do some writing. *Once Upon a Picnic* by John Prater (Walker Books) incorporates several traditional story characters into a simple story about a picnic. There is a lot of detail to find in the pictures and talk about.

Key vocabulary

The names of the story characters, such as Red Riding Hood, the Gingerbread Man, the troll, the three Billy Goats Gruff, the giant, the wicked witch.
Run, run as fast as you can
Trip, trap, trip, trap...
I'm going to eat you for my dinner...
What big eyes/ears/teeth you've got!
Fee, fi, fo, fum...

The activity

You will need:

A copy of *Once Upon a Picnic*; copies of the traditional stories referred to – 'The Gingerbread Man', 'Little Red Riding Hood', 'The Three Billy Goats Gruff', 'The Three Bears', 'Jack and the Beanstalk', 'The Old Woman Who Lived in a Shoe', and 'Sleeping Beauty' (or 'Hansel and Gretel' for the wicked witch); paper plates or coloured paper cut into circles; felt-tipped pens or coloured pencils.

● Read some of the traditional stories referred to in *Once Upon a Picnic*. Make sure that the children are familiar with the different stories and characters.

● Then read *Once Upon a Picnic* to the children, looking carefully at the pictures and identifying the different story characters.

● Ask the children to help make some food for a picnic to which you are going to invite the different story characters. Talk about the kind of food that the characters would eat – the troll loves goat... the goats love juicy grass with wild flowers growing in it... the three bears eat porridge... the giant eats giant egg and chips!

● Give each child a circle of coloured paper for a 'plate' or a paper plate and let them choose a character to make some food for. Ask them to talk about what they have drawn and scribe their words on to a label.

● The drawings and labels can be put into a book. The children can write their names as authors of the book, which should be put in the book corner for the children to read together, with their parents or carers, or members of the nursery staff.

To become competent readers, children need a lot of experience making books, making marks in books, sharing books with adults and children and talking about stories.

The children can help to make food for a picnic to which they can invite different story characters.

● Children can make invitations, inviting story characters to a picnic. This encourages them to think about *when* the picnic will happen, and *where*. You could adapt the song *Mr Bear, Mr Bear won't you come to tea?*, and invite Goldilocks, or Baby Bear or Ugly Troll...

Assessment

● Do the children know the traditional stories?

● Do the children behave like readers, holding a book and turning the pages one at a time? Do they know which is the front and which is the back of a book? Do they know that a book has a title and an author?

● Can the children explain what they want to write on a label? Do they have the confidence to write – mark making, writing random letter shapes, or moving towards independent writing? Can they write their name?

● Can the children talk about the detail in the pictures? Can they point to the print and know that it tells the story? Can they look at the pictures and make up their own story from the pictures, using story language?

Evidence of the children's learning

The children were introduced to this activity through a range of traditional stories. For some of them, this was the first time that they had encountered these stories, while others were very familiar with the sequence of events, the characters and the story language.

By the end of the activity, they were able to identify the different story characters in the pictures and talk about the stories that they appeared in. Some were able to talk about the food that the different characters would like. Other children wanted to make food for their own chosen characters.

Differentiating the activity

For children who have not come across the traditional stories before, it is helpful to focus on one story and make sure that they get to know it well. They can then use their experience to join in appropriately.

Children who have had a wide experience of the stories can be extended by talking in more detail about the characters, by retelling the stories and by encouraging them to use phrases from the stories in their own book making.

Adults can help children to express themselves clearly. They can act as a model of a writer, by scribing the children's words, talking about letter-sound correspondence, encouraging them to 'have a go' and helping the more confident writers to form the letter shapes correctly. Have samples of writing in different scripts, on food packets and display labels.

Extension activities

● Cook food from different cultures. Make food and drinks with different textures, flavours and smells. Use fresh spices, food colourings and flavourings. Have a tasting and smelling table to extend children's experiences and their vocabulary in describing smells, tastes and textures.

● Have a shop or restaurant as a role-play area and encourage the children to write labels, signs, menus and shopping lists.

● Make a shopping list for the troll... the giant... the three bears...

● Write recipes for the wicked witch.

● Talk about children's likes and dislikes. Make drawings of their favourite – and not so favourite – food!

● Write invitations to a picnic.

● Use scrap paper and card to write shopping lists, recipes, labels and price tickets for food.

The children talked about story characters while they designed meals for them.

Working with parents

● Invite parents and younger brothers and sisters to come to a picnic at the nursery and bring a contribution of their favourite food.

● Talk to parents about the value of pointing out environmental print to their children – words on food packets, labels, posters, signs – at home and when they go shopping.

Other books to read

The Giant Jam Sandwich
by John Vernon Lord (Macmillan)

This tells how a village was plagued by wasps. The villagers all worked together to make a giant jam sandwich, and they trapped the wasps inside it. The story is written in verse, and children can be encouraged to join in, by predicting the final, rhyming word of each line. They can then make some giant sandwiches (by making a patchwork of smaller ones) and make some labels for the sandwiches. They can also help write and read the instructions for making sandwiches.

This is the Bear and the Picnic Lunch
by Sarah Hayes and Helen Craig (Walker Books)

I Want My Dinner!
by Tony Ross (Collins Picture Lions)

These are two simple stories. Children will enjoy the humour and can be encouraged to look at the pictures and predict what will happen next.

Once Upon a Time
by John Prater (Walker Books)

A boy is looking out of a window, bored, with nothing to do. The text tells one story, but the pictures have details involving traditional story characters which tell another story. Children can help expand on the story told in the text, by describing the action in the pictures.

The Sandwich that Max Made
by Marcia Vaughan (Shortland Publications)

This is a large book which can be used with groups of children.

Rewriting a well-known story

Intended learning

For children to become familiar with traditional stories; to retell a well-known story and develop story language; to sequence a story; to develop an awareness of audience and work as part of a group – speaking and listening.

Introduction

When children start to read, it is very helpful if they have a fund of favourite stories. This gives them a useful structure to use when they come to write their own stories and it introduces them to vibrant story language. Jack and the Beanstalk has a simple structure, with repetitive action, and the opportunity for children to join in with repeated, rhythmic phrases.

The following activity works best with a group of around ten children. Working in groups encourages children to take turns and listen, to watch and respond to others. The work on this case study was undertaken over several group sessions.

Key vocabulary

Jack, Jack's mother, the bag of gold, the beanstalk, the giant, the giant's wife, the hen that lays golden eggs, the magic beans, the magic harp, the old man;
Fee fi fo fum
I smell the blood of an Englishman
Be he alive or be he dead
I'll grind his bones to make my bread

The activity

You will need:

A large, rectangular sheet of paper; a variety of thick and thin felt-tipped pens in a range of colours; a copy of Jack and the Beanstalk.

● While many children will know the story of Jack and the Beanstalk, it will be new to others, especially those who have English as a second language. Therefore, introduce the story over several sessions. Read it to them, talking about the characters, then go over it again to see if the children can sequence the events and remember the main characters.

● Once they are familiar with the story, all the children can contribute to a large picture which shows the different elements of the story. This is an opportunity to discuss relative size and positional language. The beanstalk could link the house and the castle. Children who are not yet doing representational drawings can help to draw the leaves and beans hanging from the beanstalk.

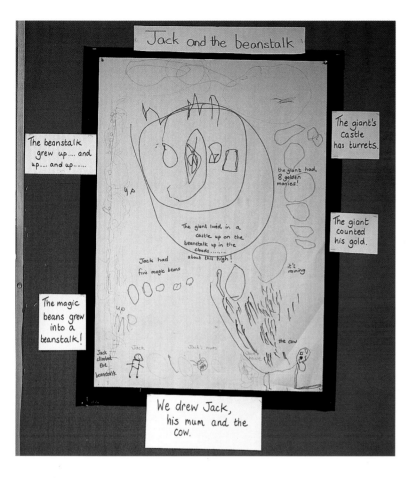

Jack and the beanstalk

The beanstalk grew up.... and up..... and up.......

The giant's castle has turrets.

the giant had 8 golden monies!

up

The giant lived in a castle up on the beanstalk up in the clouds........ about this high!

The giant counted his gold.

Jack had five magic beans

it's raining

The magic beans grew into a beanstalk!

up

the cow

Jack climbed the beanstalk

Jack

Jack's mum

We drew Jack, his mum and the cow.

The children can tell the story of Jack and the Beanstalk to each other and to adults in the nursery, using their drawings as a prompt.

● At the bottom of the paper, various children can draw Jack, Jack's mother, the cow and the old man, and the magic beans. At the top of the page, different children can draw the giant, the giant's wife, the bag of gold, the hen and the harp. The children can draw or make some gold coins, counting each one carefully. Yellow sticky paper could be used for this.

● During these drawing stages, ask the children to share their ideas about the story. What do they think the giant might look like? What would the castle look like? What does Jack's mother look like? Talk about how to make her look cross; this will help them to think about the characters in the story.

● This group picture can then be used to give children a structure to retell the story together. As they retell it, the teacher can act as scribe, providing a model of a writer, and as a model of a reader when the finished story is read back to them. Encourage the children to use narrative, description and speech in the story.

● Make a story board with pictures from the story to focus children's attention when retelling the story. Use the story and the story board to teach or reinforce vocabulary.

Assessment

● Do the children show familiarity with the story?

● Can they join in with the story, showing they have developed story language? Many of the children will be able to join in with the refrain: "Fee fi fo fum...." and Jack climbed "up and up and up and up". Some children will be starting to use conventions of story language, such as: "Once upon a time", "long, long ago" and "and that was the end of the giant!"

● Can the children sequence the story?

● Can they retell the story?

● Have the children developed an awareness of audience?

Evidence of the children's learning

The children all contributed to a large picture of the story, during which time they shared their ideas of what the people, places and objects might look like. One child drew the castle at the top of the paper. He became very enthusiastic and drew his version of some turrets. Another child drew Jack's house at the bottom. We were very impressed with some of the drawings, which demonstrated good observational skills.

Differentiating the activity

All of the children involved in the activity should show some familiarity with the story of Jack and the Beanstalk. Asking some to give a simple answer to questions such as, 'What did the old man give Jack?' ('Magic beans') will suffice.

Others will need prompt questions in order to sequence two or more events. For example:
'Jack met the old man.'
'...and what happened then?'
'He gave Jack the magic beans.'
'... and what did Jack give him?'

Not all children will have the speaking skills to tell the story, but they may be able to point to pictures and use key words to say what happened next.

Some children may be able to sequence a complex string of events and tell the story themselves. As they have more practice at telling stories, they will become aware of the need to make their meaning clear to the reader or listener. They can be helped by giving them prompt questions and modelling an unambiguous phrase:
'He went down the road.'
'Who?'
'Him.'
'The giant?'
'No, Jack!'
'So Jack went down the road?'
'Yes!'

Some children will be able to make their own books, and make up their own version of the story. Making books helps them to understand how books work, that they have a front and back, and pages which you turn to tell the story. They could number the pages and either begin to write the story or have an adult scribe their words.

Jack went home with the beans. Jack's mum threw them out of the window. She was furious and angry and cross and mad and she stamped her feet and she frowned and she screamed and she sent Jack to bed without any supper.

Part of the children's version of Jack and the Beanstalk, scribed by their teacher.

Extension activities

● The children could act out the story of Jack and the Beanstalk. A large pair of boots and an adult's jacket could be enough to distinguish the giant from the other characters!

● They could make a large group picture of the giant. One child could draw the face and others add the eyes, a nose, a mouth, hair and so on. They could make another picture of the giant's wife, and decide on names for them both.

● Planting beans gives children a chance to experience different textures and to develop fine motor skills, pouring water, handling seeds, spooning compost and filling pots. They will need to care for their plant, watering it and watching it grow.

● Make a beanstalk grow up the wall of the nursery. Let the children draw leaves, cut them out and write their names on them. Each child could stick their leaf on the beanstalk to make it grow.

● Act out and make group pictures of other traditional stories.

Working with parents

● If possible, have copies of traditional stories available for children to take home and read with their families.

● If you have families who come from other countries, try and persuade the parents to come in and tell some of their traditional stories.

● Encourage parents to stay and share books with children in the book area.

Other books to read

Hairy Tales and Nursery Crimes
by Michael Rosen (Young Lions)

This has versions of familiar tales and rhymes, adapted with humour. For example 'The Silly Ghosts Gruff, Goldilocks and the Wee Bears'. Children enjoy the element of surprise, and might enjoy making their own silly versions. Learning the rules and breaking them helps children to understand the structure of stories.

Jim and the Beanstalk
by Raymond Briggs (Puffin)

This book helps children to think about "what happens next?" It carries the original story on to when the giant is an old man.

The True Story of the Three Little Pigs
by Jon Scieszka (Puffin)

This tells a well-known story from a different perspective and encourages children to take different viewpoints in other stories. How did the troll feel when he saw the first Billy Goat Gruff... and the third Billy Goat Gruff? How did The Ugly Sisters feel when Cinderella married the prince? Tell the story of Little Red Riding Hood from the wolf's point of view.

Personalising a story

Intended learning

For the children to follow a simple story structure; to think about 'what happens next?'; to develop story language; to learn that stories have authors and illustrators.

Introduction

Goodnight Owl by Pat Hutchins (Picture Puffin) is a story with a simple structure and repeated phrases, 'and Owl couldn't sleep...', which children pick up quickly. In this activity, we used the story to encourage children to draw pictures based on their own experiences. A story was developed from their drawings, helping them to use pictures to 'read' a story, and giving them a basis from which to make up their own story language.

Key vocabulary

goodnight, owl, 'owl couldn't sleep'

The activity

You will need:

A copy of *Goodnight Owl*; a large blank book, made from sheets of coloured paper stapled together (for making a group book); some drawing paper cut to fit on the pages of the home-made book; a selection of coloured pencils, crayons and felt-tipped pens; some small blank books for individual children to write their own stories in.

● Look at the cover of *Goodnight Owl* and ask the children for suggestions as to what it is about. Before you turn a page, ask them what might happen next. All the suggestions can be the basis for a discussion.

● Read the book and discuss with the children the fact that people sleep at night and owls sleep in the day. The children might start to join in with repeated phrases in the story: 'and owl couldn't sleep.' If this is encouraged, they will start to use similar phrases in their own versions of the story.

● Encourage them to look at detail in the pictures to enrich their understanding of the story, and to develop their vocabulary, as they describe what happens. Discuss the fact that stories have authors and illustrators. Help them to recognise several books by one author/illustrator such as John Burningham and Shirley Hughes.

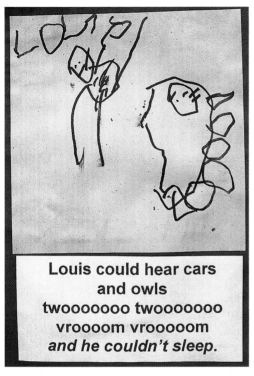

Louis could hear cars and owls
twooooooo twooooooo
vroooom vrooooom
and he couldn't sleep.

Agnes could hear a squirrel
kkkkkkkkkkkkkkkkk
and she couldn't sleep.

Daniel could hear his clock tick tock tick tock
and he couldn't sleep.

Hari's in his bunkbed. He's having a bit of a nap and
trying to sleep.

● Talk about the sounds that the children hear at night when they are in bed. Encourage them to contribute an idea, helping children with limited spoken language.

● Ask them to draw something that they can hear at night – the radio, the television, a dog barking, motorbikes, a baby crying, the wind in the trees...

● Put the drawings into a book. Scribe their words under their pictures while they watch.

● Give the story a title, such as 'Goodnight Children', and write their names on the cover, as the authors.

● Encourage the children to read the book that they have helped to write and talk about who drew the different pictures.

The children's pictures and the repeated phrase encouraged them to read the story that they helped to write.

Assessment

● Can the children talk about what happens in the story?

● Can they talk about what might happen on the next page while they are listening to the story?

● Can they sequence the events in the story?

● Can they contribute their own ideas of something that might happen next?

● Can they help make up a story using appropriate story language?

Evidence of children's learning

With some prompting, many of the children came up with a phrase in story language, imitating *Goodnight Owl*.
'The baby was crying and Daniel couldn't sleep.'
'The dog was barking and Nabilah couldn't sleep.'
'The motorbikes went brooooooooommmmm and Maisie couldn't sleep.'
'The radio went da da da da da da da da and Stephen couldn't sleep.'
'The wind went wooooooooooooooo and Hamza couldn't sleep.'

The children talked about how the story might end, for example,
'In the morning the children woke Mum and Dad up. 'We want our breakfast!'
...and Mum and Dad couldn't sleep.'

Differentiating the activity

For children who have difficulty with sequencing, make storyboard pictures to retell the story.

Read and retell other simple stories. *Peace at Last* by Jill Murphy follows on well from *Goodnight Owl*, as it is about a bear who can't sleep because of noises in the house and garden at night.

For children who have difficulty saying what might keep people awake at night, make a tape with different sounds – a dog barking, a car passing, a clock ticking, a baby crying, a cat miaowing. Play it to them and see if they can identify the sounds. Cards with pictures matching the sounds will help children who find this difficult.

Some children could make individual books based on the story. This is a chance to talk about letter/sound correspondence, as an adult scribes the child's story – especially when it comes to writing the sounds that the children can hear, such as 'brooooomm' and 'creeeak..'

Use musical instruments to tell stories with sound accompaniments. Simple stories can be retold, using a wooden block and a beater for a clock, or a rainstick for the sound of rain, or the sea. With support, some children might be able to make up a simple story of their own, using instruments.

Extension activities

● Make signs saying BE QUIET, NO TALKING, KITCHEN, PAINTS and so on.

● Read other books by Pat Hutchins and talk about similarities in the style of illustration. Make a display of her books and talk about authors and illustrators. Look at some books with different styles of illustration, such as those by Quentin Blake.

● Make a large wall frieze. The children can draw or paint the birds and the tree. Place the birds on the tree with the words of the story, so that the story can be followed from the picture.

Working with parents

● Encourage parents to read the group book, individual stories and the frieze story together.

● Suggest that parents play 'I hear with my little ear... something that goes 'tweet'... something that goes 'creak'...'

● Have books by Pat Hutchins for children to borrow and read at home. For example, *My Best Friend, The Wind Blew, Happy Birthday, Sam, Tidy Titch, Three Star Billy, Don't Forget the Bacon!, The Doorbell Rang* (All Puffin).

Other books to read

Peace at Last
by Jill Murphy (Macmillan)

This tells the story of a bear who can't sleep. He moves around the house and garden, trying to find somewhere quiet and peaceful but there are noises everywhere. This story can help to stimulate discussion on the sounds that children hear at night.

Lullaby Hullabaloo
by Mick Inkpen (Hodder and Stoughton)

This can be used to introduce simple phonic work, where appropriate, and children can compare the different sounds heard in the different stories.

Owl Babies
by Martin Waddell (Walker)

This is another story about owls. It describes how the babies feel as they wait for their mother to return from her night's hunting trip.

Left: One child wrote his own version of *Goonight Owl*, adapting the title.

Sequencing a story

Intended learning

For the children to understand the difference between print and pictures; to sequence a story and to make predictions – what happens next?; to learn that a story has an author; to work as part of a group – taking turns, speaking and listening; to learn some specific vocabulary.

Introduction

Rosie's Walk by Pat Hutchins (The Bodley Head) can be used effectively to introduce children to a simple story structure. This activity took place at a group time with ten children. Several of the children knew the story already and all the children had been on a recent visit to a farm with the nursery. During the activity, the children drew a map of Rosie's route around the farm, while the teacher scribed their words. Then they used the pictures on the map to 'read' the story.

Key vocabulary

across, around, beehives, fence, fox, haycock, mill, over, past, pond, Rosie the hen, through, under, yard

The activity

You will need:
A copy of *Rosie's Walk*; a large piece of paper; some thick and thin felt-tipped pens.

● Have some model farm animals out for children to play with. Talk about the animals that live on a farm.

● Talk about the author. Some of the children may know that Pat Hutchins has written other books. Look at the pictures on the cover and ask the children to guess what might happen in the story. Look at the inside front cover and then introduce the children to the vocabulary that they would come across in the story – especially unfamiliar words such as haycock.

● Then read the story. Before turning the pages, encourage the children to read the pictures and predict 'what might happen next?' Talking about details in the pictures helps the children to see that the pictures carry a lot of the story that isn't told in the words. It is important to give children time to look closely at the pictures before turning the page. They will start to come up with their own ideas about what happens next.

● When they are familiar with the story, start to make a map of Rosie's route around the farm. Using the map to retell the story gives the children a structure from which they can make up their own story language, or remember the words of the text.

● Finally, let the children retell the story and trace Rosie's route around the farm. Reading and re-reading stories helps them to contribute to the story as they become familiar with it.

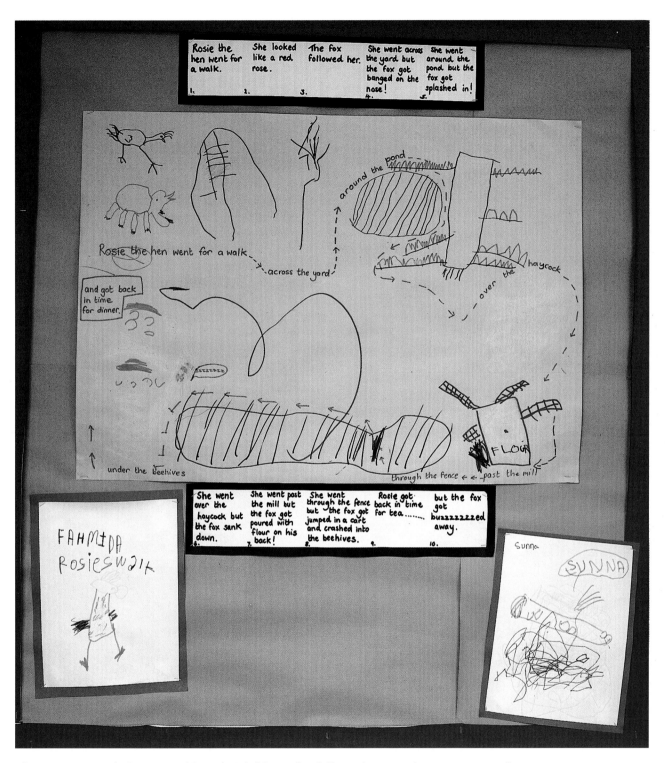

The sequence of the story 'Rosie's Walk' can be followed using the pictures and arrows.

Assessment

● Do the children understand the difference between print and pictures? Can they use the pictures to talk about the characters and the story? Do they behave like readers, pretending to read a story using their own story language? Do they understand that the print carries the words that tell the story?

● Can the children follow the sequence of events in a story and remember what is going to happen next? Can they use the pictures to make predictions about what might happen? Do they have a sense of excitement, wanting to turn the pages to see what happens next?

● Can the children name any authors and the books that they have written? Do children want to write their names on their own stories, or contributions to group stories?

● Can the children take turns talking and listening in a group? Do they enjoy helping to produce a group story?

● Can the children use the vocabulary of position accurately and appropriately?

Evidence of children's learning

On first reading the book, the children spotted the fox immediately, and decided that he was 'hungry'.

As they drew the map, the children drew Rosie, the fox and the hen house in the top left-hand corner. They then drew the yard with the rake, the pond, the haycock, the mill, the fence and the beehives in sequence around the paper. They then drew in Rosie's route. Some children were able to use the appropriate vocabulary, 'Rosie went over, around, across', 'until Rosie returned to the hen house – safely!'

Differentiating the activity

Writing a group story is a good way of developing speaking and listening skills. It also helps children to feel that their contribution is valued.

Children's use of positional vocabulary will improve as they become familiar with the text. Tracing Rosie's route on the children's map helps them to use the vocabulary accurately.

Make pictures of the fox and the hen, and the main places that Rosie goes past on her walk to use to retell the story. The picture will help reinforce the vocabulary, and the hen can be moved as needed – over, under, around...

A zigzag book retelling the story will help children to see the sequence of events more easily. Cards could be made showing Rosie at different places in the farm, and the children could sequence these.

Extension activities

● Some children could make books about themselves, called 'Sonia's Walk' or 'Iqbal's Walk', drawing pictures of the places they see as they walk to nursery school or to the park.

● Sing 'Old Macdonald has a farm' and 'There's a fox in a box'. For the latter, the words are:

There's a fox in a box (in my little bed)
(3 times)
And there isn't much room for me.

There's a bear with brown hair...

There's a parrot with a carrot...

You can make up your own verses.

● Make a model of Rosie's farm from boxes or Lego.

● Use outdoor equipment to go on a walk like Rosie's, over, under, and through...

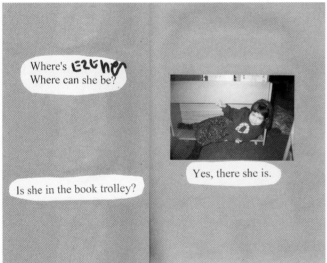

Make a lift-the-flap book featuring the children in the class and using positional language – under, behind, in and so on.

Working with parents

● Encourage parents to share books with their children in the book area, and talk about the value of telling stories as well as reading them.

● Encourage the children to show their parents the map, and to tell their parents the story from the map.

● Ask parents to play a game as they walk to nursery, talking about things that they pass – 'We are walking through the gate, over the grass, under the bridge...'

Other books to read

The Little Red Hen
by Tony Bradman and Jenny Williams (Methuen)

This is another story that has simple sequencing of events.

Fantastic Mr Fox
by Roald Dahl (Collins)

This story presents the fox as the hero, not the villain.

On the Way Home
by Jill Murphy (Macmillan)

This is another story about a journey. On the way home Claire hurts her knee and she imagines different reasons for this having happened. It has a simple structure and lends itself to simple adaptation.

We're Going on a Bear Hunt
by Michael Rosen and Helen Oxenbury (Walker Books)

A picture book of the well-known activity story.

Writing in imaginative play

Intended learning

For the children to recognise that print carries a message – reading and writing labels, signs, letters, instructions, messages; to follow instructions; to extend oral language in play.

Introduction

We decided to hold a 'pirates day', culminating in a picnic, to stimulate the children's imaginative play and encourage both spoken and written language. Dressing-up clothes and props help stimulate vocabulary development and more complex interactive language, as the children create imaginary worlds. The songs and rhymes encourage listening skills and help develop concentration. They also help children to learn different language patterns and sounds.

Key vocabulary

cabin boy, captain, grog, 'land ahoy', pirate, 'swab the decks', weevil biscuits

The activity

You will need:

Card and paper to make simple pirate hats; eye patches; maps and flags made by the children; thick and thin felt-tipped pens, coloured pencils and crayons; card for signs, labels and invitations; songs about pirates:

'When I was one I sucked my thumb,
The day I went to sea.
I jumped aboard a pirate ship and the captain said to me
'We're sailing this way, that way, forwards and backwards, over the Irish Sea
A bottle of rum to fill my tum and that's the life for me.'

When I was two I buckled my shoe ...'
Continue this, making up verses for the different ages.

● Introduce the idea of a pirate day at group time, through stories, such as those listed over the page, and by discussing what pirates wear, what they might eat, where they live, the kinds of names they have and the jobs they do on the ships. Use props to stimulate the children's imagination.

● The pirate stories can be read at several group times before pirate day and the children could talk about pirate stories and videos that they know, such as Peter Pan and Hook.

● Help the children to write a joint letter to their parents telling them about the pirate day and asking if the children can dress up as pirates on that day.

● Talk about the kinds of food and drink that pirates like. Help them to write labels and recipes for the food and drink: weevil biscuits, mouldy jam sandwiches, grog and so on.

● The day before pirate day and on the day itself, the children can make pirate hats, flags with a skull and cross bones to fly on the pirate ship, treasure maps with instructions telling the reader where to find the treasure. Making these requires children to listen carefully and follow instructions in a sequence.

● They can also write messages to put inside plastic bottles ('Help, I've been captured by pirates. Come and save me.') and large signs to hang around the nursery (JOLLY ROGER, BEWARE SHARKS, PIRATES ONLY.)

Telling an adult what they want to write helps them to see that writing is an important way of communicating ideas and messages. They can then be encouraged to write without an adult and read back their writing. At this stage, the aim is for them to remember the sense of what they have written rather than to read accurately.

● Lots of child-initiated activity can result, such as making pirate ships and swords.

● Different areas of the nursery can be set up for role play, with appropriate dressing-up clothes available. Moustaches can be painted on with face paints (check with parents first to make sure that children aren't allergic to face paints). The role-play areas could include a 'pirate ship' outside, with a plank from a climbing frame, so that children can 'walk the plank' and a small boat in the sand pit with buckets and spades and a source of water nearby.

● Bring the children together for group time and tell them that there is some treasure hidden in the garden. Show them a very simple map of the garden with a large x marked on it. They can work out where the treasure is hidden, and go to find it. The 'treasure' could be a plastic chest with sandwiches, biscuits and drink inside, which can be shared out at a picnic in the garden.

● Finally, sing some pirate songs. A lot of children will listen and join in with actions to begin with. Playing around with familiar tunes and making up words helps them to think about rhyming and rhythmic patterns, appropriate language and to build up a store of well-known tunes.

Even pirates need to be able to read and write!

Assessment

● Writing for a purpose – Do children show an understanding that marks on paper can have meaning? Can they make marks on paper and 'read' their writing to an adult? Can they 'talk' a message for an adult to scribe? Can they write recognisable letter shapes, with some understanding of letter-sound correspondence?

● Following instructions – Can children work in a group or individually, following a sequence of instructions?

● Can the children follow a simple pattern in a song – verse, chorus, verse, chorus? Can they remember tunes from well-known songs? Can they help to make up new words to well-known tunes? Do they join in with actions and words?

● Developing oral language in play – Do the children play imaginatively – in a group? or individually? Do they use appropriate language in their imaginative play – in a group? individually? Can they talk to adults about their imaginative play?
What experiences are reflected by the language they use in their play?

Evidence of the children's learning

The children enjoyed thinking up names for the pirates' food, such as dead man's leg sandwiches and shark sandwiches, and then writing labels for them. Some children were very good at thinking of messages to put in a bottle; others wrote signs independently, such as HEP (help) and JER (Jolly Roger).

Differentiating the activity

Make some storyboard pictures, with characters from the stories: a pirate ship, a pirate's cat, a treasure chest and so on. Storyboard pictures provide a stimulus for discussing simple stories with children who have a limited experience of books and making up their own stories. They can also be the starting point for individual or group stories, with an adult scribing the children's words.

Dressing up clothes and props help stimulate vocabulary development and more complex language.

The songs and rhymes encourage listening skills and help develop concentration. They also help children to learn different language patterns and sounds. Some children will be beginning to build up a simple repertoire of songs. Other children will be able to draw on their experiences or to play with rhyming words to create new verses for songs.

Right: Children helped to illustrate a pirate recipe!

Extension activities

● Make pirate books – information books, story books, books in the shape of pirate hats or pirate ships.

● Make a map of the nursery garden, or one of the rooms. Mark on key places. Make maps showing how you come to the nursery. Mark on them some things that you see on the way.

● Make a simple board game, for example using a dice to move pirates ships from a port to a treasure island. If you meet a sea monster, go back two squares. A strong wind blows the ship forward.

Working with parents

● The letter that the children send to their parents about Pirate Day makes a link between the nursery and home and helps involve parents in the learning that takes place in the nursery.

● A photographic display of Pirate Day can be used to explain how the different curriculum areas are covered, and how children learn through play.

● Parents can be invited to join in with the pirate picnic and songs.

Other books to read

Pirate Poll
by Susan Hill (Puffin)

Captain Abdul's Pirate School
by Colin McNaughton (Walker Books)

Mudge the Smuggler
by John Ryan (Macmillan)

Captain Pugwash
stories by John Ryan (Puffin)

The Pirate and the Pig
by Frank Rodgers (Puffin)

Captain Teachum's Buried Treasure
by Korky Paul and Peter Carter (OUP)

These stories will stimulate children's imaginative play, by offering models of different types of behaviour. The different stories challenge the stereotype of the tough, masculine pirate.

The stories will extend the children's spoken language by suggesting phrases and situations which they can use in their play.

Writing at the post office

Intended learning

For the children to become familiar with traditional stories; to understand that print carries a message; to write for a purpose – letter writing; to learn the conventions of letter writing.

Introduction

We used traditional stories as a starting point for encouraging letter writing. Many children knew the stories well and had absorbed them into their play. This activity provided an opportunity for other children to get to know new stories or to become more familiar with stories that they knew a little. The activity was initially teacher directed at group time, but children began to write letters as part of their play during the session, showing some independence and awareness of the purpose of letter writing.

Key vocabulary

The names of the story characters: Goldilocks, the giant, Jack, Red Riding Hood, the three bears, the three billy goats Gruff, the troll; words for letter writing – dear, love from, to; the children's own names; address, envelope, post box, postman, stamp

The activity

You will need:
For the post office: paper, envelopes, forms, rubber stamps, old stamps and glue sticks, sticky labels, posters. Different versions of traditional stories – books, tapes, puppets. Resources for role-play areas: three different-sized bowls, chairs and beds for the three bears' house; a 'bridge' for the story of the 'Three Billy Goats Gruff', a castle for the giant in 'Jack and the Beanstalk'; a large piece of paper and thick felt-tipped pens; Goldilocks' shoe.

● Make a display of books of traditional stories and story tapes. Set up role-play areas inside and outside to encourage play based on traditional stories. Concentrate on one story at a time. Set up a post office for role play.

● Read the story of Goldilocks and the Three Bears at group time. At the end of the story, tell the children that Goldilocks had left a shoe behind at the three bears' house, and suggest that they write to Goldilocks and tell her.

● Provide a large piece of paper and discuss with the children how to start a letter, the message in the letter, and how to finish a letter. Scribe their words for them, providing a model of a writer, and then encourage them to add their names to the three bears' names at the end of the letter.

● Use the computer keyboard and 'Write' program to write letters. Software is available that enables a letter template to be set up so that children can input their own details.

- Discuss how the letter would get to Goldilocks – they need an envelope, a stamp, the address and a letter box.

- Show them the post office area and the resources available for writing their own letters. Make sure adult support is available at the post office area during the rest of the session.

- Intervention can include scribing their messages, asking them to 'read' the marks they have made, suggesting messages that could be sent, such as to the school secretary asking for more envelopes, giving help with putting the letters into the envelopes and writing the name on the envelope.

- Encourage them to deliver their letters to people in the nursery.

The children produced a lot of spontaneous writing which provided opportunities for adult intervention and future planning.

Assessment

● Can the children make up their own letters by following the simple structure provided by the teacher in the letter to Goldilocks: by talking their message? by writing their message?

● Do the children understand why we write and send letters?

● Can they write key words needed for letter writing and their own name at the end of a letter?

Evidence of the children's learning

A lot of children became very interested in the Post Office area. Some of them folded pieces of paper and put them inside different-sized envelopes. Others made marks on paper, put the paper inside an envelope and gave it to someone specific. Some children wrote a name on their envelopes.

Differentiating the activity

Some children will make marks on paper, put the paper in an envelope, make marks on the envelope and post the letter. They might be able to tell someone what they have written, but for some children, the message might not be important. Playing with paper and envelopes can be an important part of the process of copying adult behaviour, a stage that allows children to experiment as they develop an understanding of what letter writing involves.

Some children will write a name, but no message, on a piece of paper, and put it in an envelope. They know the letter is for someone, but they haven't understood that letters are a way of sending a message.

Some children will have a clear idea of the message they want to send. They will need varying degrees of help to write the message.

Some children will have learned the conventional spellings for words, such as dear, to and love from. Some of them might be using their understanding of letter/sound correspondence to attempt their own spellings.

Extension activities

● Encourage the children to write to characters from different stories and rhymes, such as from Jack to the giant and from the Billy Goats Gruff to their mother telling her about the troll.

● Help children to write a postcard to themselves or someone in their family, take them to a post office to buy a stamp, and let the children put the card in the post box. They can wait for the card to arrive at their home!

● Hang a plastic spider called Incy Wincy, up in a corner of the nursery and ask the children to write and ask him questions: Have you got any brothers and sisters? What do you eat? Where did you live before you came to nursery? Help Incy Wincy to write back!

● Visit a post office to buy some stamps and make a collection of stamps from different places.

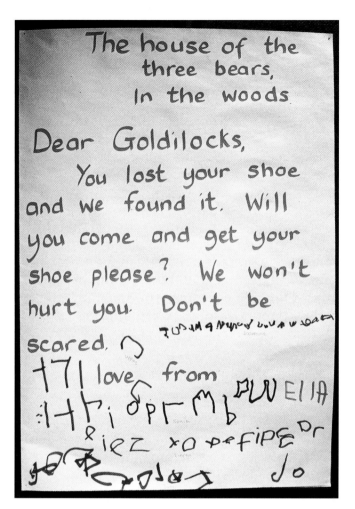

> The house of the three bears,
> In the woods
>
> Dear Goldilocks,
>   You lost your shoe and we found it. Will you come and get your shoe please? We won't hurt you. Don't be scared.
>
> love from

The teacher scribed the children's words and then they all had a go at writing their names.

● Help children to send letters and notes to other children and adults in the nursery. They might be functional messages to the secretary ("Please can we have some more paper clips?"), or more interesting letters to each other ("Dear Red Group, We have just found some woodlice under a log in the garden. Would you like to come and see them?")

Working with parents

● Ask parents to help when you visit a post office.

● Encourage parents to help their children send a card to the nursery when they go on holiday or if they visit somewhere special at the weekend.

● If you have families from other countries, try and write to a relative who lives abroad, and hope that they will write back.

Other books to read

Dear Zoo
by Rod Campbell (Puffin)

This is a very simple story of a child who writes to a zoo to ask them to send him an animal. It can be used as the starting point for letter-writing.

A Message for Santa
by Hiawyn Oram and Tony Ross (Andersen Press)

Again, a story that can be used to introduce message- and letter-writing.

King Rollo's Letter and other stories
by David McKee (Beaver Books)

King Rollo writes a letter to himself, then eagerly awaits its arrival.

The *Jolly Postman* series
by Janet and Alan Ahlberg (Heinemann)

All these books provide a delightful stimulus to writing and sending letters and cards.

Writing at the railway station

Intended learning

For the children to understand that print carries a message; to learn the conventions of some different types of writing; to begin to form letter shapes; to begin to understand the correspondence between some letter shapes and their sounds.

Introduction

Well-resourced role-play areas provide valuable opportunities for children to learn about writing and reading in the context of imaginative play. The role-play area for this case study was set up and adapted over a period of a week or so, inside the nursery and in the garden.

Key vocabulary

cafe, driver, guard, information, newsagent, station, tickets, train

The activity

You will need:

Dressing-up clothes: jackets, a guard's hat, clothes for people working in the station cafe; suitcases and rucksacks for the passengers; a flag and a whistle for the guard. Resources for a ticket and information office: tickets, timetables, leaflets, posters, a telephone, diaries, pads, small books, paper and card, a variety of pencils, felt tips and crayons. Resources for a station cafe: plates, cups, bowls, cutlery, pretend food, menus and a price list, pads for taking orders. Resources for a station newsagents: magazines, books, a till, plastic coins. Climbing equipment for making a train: planks, tyres, A-frames, boxes, milk crates, chairs.

● If possible, introduce the activity by taking some children on a short train ride, perhaps to visit another nursery. The children could help write a letter to the nursery asking if they could come and visit them.

● Talk with the children about their experiences if they have been on a train journey – where they have been, how long the journey took and comparisons with other forms of travel.

● Talk about the people who work at the station – train drivers, guards, ticket collectors, people who sell tickets or work at the information office, people who work in the cafe or newsagents.

● Read stories about train journeys, such as *Oi! Get Off My Train* by John Burningham (Jonathan Cape Ltd) and *The Train Ride* by June Crebbin (Walker Books).

● Set up a railway station and create a train with large blocks, tables or cardboard boxes. A steering wheel and a guard's hat will be enough to stimulate children to use the structure as a train! Set up a ticket and information office where children can get tickets and information about train times and routes. Create a cafe area with small tables and chairs. Magazines and books can be displayed in a 'newsagents', together with a till.

● Writing can be encouraged in different ways. A variety of writing materials and different-sized pieces of paper, card and books should be available in the different areas of the 'station', providing both a stimulus and a resource for writing activities. The children should have constant access to these materials so that they can write tickets, signs or labels for suitcases.

The railway station and train encouraged lots of spontaneous writing as part of the children's imaginative play.

Assessment

● Understanding that print carries a message – Can the children suggest a meaning for signs and writing around them? Do they make marks on paper and talk about what they have written? Do they choose to write for a purpose in their play?

● Do the children differentiate between various types of writing? Can they make a sensible guess at the meaning of the words on a sign, a label, a ticket, a letter..? Do they choose appropriate paper, card or books for different types of writing? For example, small pieces of paper for tickets, a book for a timetable, a large piece of paper for a sign, paper and an envelope for a letter. Do they choose to write for a range of purposes in their play? Do they understand some of the conventions of different types of writing? For example, large writing on signs, a mixture of letters and numbers on a timetable or a ticket, pictures and writing on a poster.

● Do the children form recognisable letter shapes when they write? Can they differentiate between letters and numbers?

Evidence of children's learning

Both adults and children provided models of writers and readers. Adults made suggestions of types of writing that children could do. They scribed the children's words and they helped with their independent writing. Because the writing materials were continually available, many children used them freely in their play, while other children played side by side, observing the writing that was taking place.

Differentiating the activity

Children need a lot of practice! Resources should be constantly available and the role-play area should be set up and be available over a period of time. They need to be given time to move from the stage of simple experimentation with materials to using writing materials imaginatively in their play.

Observation of children's play and adult support will be needed to help children at an appropriate level.

If you have children for whom English is a second language, try and have signs written in scripts representing their first languages.

To help children who have difficulty communicating verbally, sing songs about train journeys – 'Train is a-comin', 'The wheels on the train' (adapting the words from 'The wheels on the bus'...)

Extension activities

● Imaginative play can be extended with a train set and Duplo, Lego or Playpeople. The children can be encouraged to take a model train to a farm, or a zoo, or a castle, writing signs for stations, and tickets for the passengers.

● Make a book about the things you can see from a train window. The children can draw trees, cows, houses, parks, cars and so on.

● Make biscuits using train cutters and make sandwiches to 'sell' in the station cafe.

● Write stories about journeys, or about family holidays.

The children drew pictures and talked about things that they might see from a train window.

Working with parents

● Parents may be able to help if you can organise a train ride for the children.

● Suggest that parents help their children to write a postcard and send it to the nursery when they go on holiday.

● Suggest that parents save tickets from bus or train journeys and show them to their children.

Other books to read

Mr Gumpy's Outing
by John Burningham (Puffin)

This book can be used to stimulate writing for different purposes. Children can write invitations from Mr Gumpy to different people or animals, inviting them to come on an outing. They can write tickets for different outings and signs and labels for car, train or boat rides. They can write thank you letters to Mr Gumpy.

Teddybears Take the Train
by Susanna Gretz and Alison Sage (Hippo books)

In this book, the bears pass the time playing a memory game, each adding to a growing list of things they took on their journey.

Are We Nearly There?
Louis Baum (Magnet)

This describes a small boy's journey on a train with his dad, to his mum's house. There is a lot for children to talk about, from the things the boy can see from the train window, to the emotions involved in such a journey.

Writing recipes and shopping lists

Intended learning

For the children to learn that print carries a message; to write for different purposes: lists, labels, recipes; to learn to sequence; to form letter shapes and match words; to use initial sounds of words and recognise key words; to learn directionality.

Introduction

This activity took place at group times and during the nursery morning and afternoon sessions. A cooking activity arising from Chinese New Year celebrations was designed to give children an understanding of some of the reasons why we write, and to give them the opportunity to practise writing in a context. The activity began with a structured element: writing shopping lists together, going shopping, writing a recipe. Then an unstructured role-play area was set up to give children a chance to experiment and practise writing as part of their imaginative play.

Key vocabulary

chop, chopping board, chopsticks, cook, eat, fry, knife, names of vegetables, pour, stir, wok; words connected with the festival of Chinese New Year

The activity

You will need:

Resources for a role-play Chinese restaurant: crockery and cutlery, including chop sticks; menus and pads for taking orders; empty packets of Chinese food; aprons for the waiters and waitresses and the chefs; a play cooker and cooking equipment, including a wok.

● Talk about familiar festivals and how they are celebrated. Ask if anyone knows about the Chinese New Year festival. Then explain that you are going to make a Chinese dish to celebrate the festival and the culture.

● Talk about different kinds of vegetables and where to get them. Sing the song 'What shall we buy at the supermarket? (3 times) ...Filling up our trolley.' (sung to the tune of 'What shall we do with the drunken sailor'). The children's suggestions for vegetables can make up the verses of the song, such as 'onions and tomatoes in our trolley'. Look at pictures and let the children handle some real vegetables. Then cut some in half and talk about colour, size, shape, texture and the children's likes and dislikes.

● Make out a shopping list with words and pictures, then write a letter and make a poster asking parents for contributions.

● Some of you could visit a local Chinese supermarket, with the parents helping. If you are lucky enough, you might have a Chinese family linked to the school who will help you.

● Ask the children to match the words on the shopping list with words on the labels in the supermarket. They could look at the writing on the till receipt and talk about the price of the vegetables. This will help with recognition of numbers in the written form.

There were opportunities for role-playing different aspects of making the stir fry. This led to some good reading and writing activities.

● During the cooking session when the teacher cooks the stir fry, the children could come and help chop vegetables. While they are chopping, remind them of the words of the rhyme:

Chop chop chop chop.
Chop off the bottom and chop off the top.
All the rest goes into the pot.
Chop chop chop chop.

Stir the stir fry, stir the stir fry.
Have a little taste.
What this stir fry needs is... an onion!
(or a carrot, or a pepper...)

● Write out a recipe for a vegetable stir fry, talking about the sequence involved in cooking. An adult can write the children's words and the children can draw pictures next-to the words and write their names. Writing and following a recipe is a useful structured activity, which helps children learn to sequence.

● Finally, let the children play in a role-play area of a Chinese restaurant, where they can eat the stir fry that they have made, and play at being waiters/waitresses, taking orders. Appropriate writing materials should be constantly available so that children can experiment with writing lists, labels, recipes and menus. Adult support can be given to help them to use writing as part of their imaginative play - by suggesting types of writing that children can do, by helping them to formulate what they want to say and by scribing their words or helping them with independent writing.

Assessment

● Do the children recognise that print carries different kinds of messages?

● Can the children form letter shapes? Can they use the initial sound of a word to identify it? Can they match words and recognise a few keywords in a context?

● Can children sequence an activity?

Evidence of children's learning

Some children knew the initial sound of some of the ingredients on their shopping list. They helped to write the list and used the initial sound to identify words on the list. Some children helped to sequence the cooking activity and then they helped to read back the recipe that the teacher had written. Many of the children experimented with writing menus, lists and taking orders in the restaurant.

Differentiating the activity

Awareness of letter-sound correspondence can be achieved by pointing out print around them, and by talking to children about letter shapes and sounds. Some children will be able to use the initial letter of a word, pictures and context to help them.

Extend vocabulary by setting up a tasting table, where they can try food with different flavours and textures. Encourage them to describe the colours, flavours and textures of the food. Make a chart showing their likes and dislikes.

Children will develop fine motor skills by using a knife, a spoon and chopsticks.

Extension activities

● Make a collection of food packets and labels from different countries, with different scripts. Vary the role-play area to include food and cooking from other ethnic groups.

● Make Ang Pow (lucky envelopes) by folding a rectangle of red paper with one curved end for the flap. Decorate it with yellow paint – printing or painting with small brushes. Traditionally, these are filled with money but you could put in foil-wrapped chocolate money or sweets. Let the children take them home.

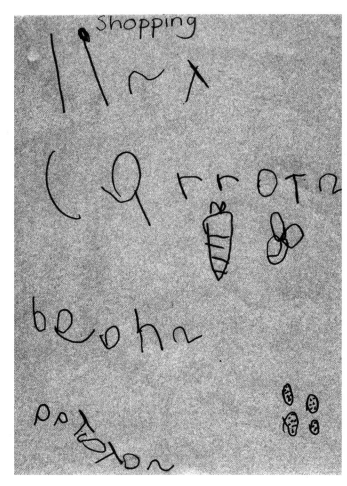

Children wrote shopping lists with adult support and spontaneously, in their play.

● The Chinese years are named after a story called 'The legend of the animals'. Twelve animals had a race across a river to decide who should have the first year named after them. Ox was winning but Rat cheated by climbing on Ox's back, then running along his back and jumping on to land first. Ox was very surprised when the Gods declared Rat the winner.

1998 The Tiger
1997 The Ox
1996 The Rat
1995 The Pig
1994 The Dog
1993 The Rooster
1992 The Monkey
1991 The Ram
1990 The Horse
1989 The Snake
1988 The Dragon
1987 The Rabbit

Make a chart with pictures of the animals, showing when the children and adults in the nursery were born.

● Learn to say Happy New Year in Chinese – Kung Hey Fat Choy.

● Cooking, washing up and eating with others helps children's social development.

Working with parents

● Chinese families with children in the nursery might come and talk about Chinese New Year. They could demonstrate Chinese writing.

● Other parents can be encouraged to come and share books with children during the session, help with cooking, or help out on the trip to the shops.

● They could look at a display or photograph book of the activity, and talk to their child about what they have been doing.

● They could make a stir fry at home – the school could photocopy the children's recipe for parents to use, and as an example of children's writing.

Other books to read

Stone Soup
by Tony Ross (Beaver Books)

Stone Soup tells how a hen tricks a wolf into doing all of her chores, while she makes 'stone soup' – adding all kinds of vegetables to improve the flavour. The wolf eats the soup, and then he is too full up to eat the hen! Children can compare the hen's recipe for stone soup with their recipe for stir fry, while they enjoy the humour of the story.

Stir Fry
by Ruth Nagrath Woodbridge (A&C Black)

Stir Fry is a simple well-illustrated information book about vegetables. It explains how we eat different parts of plants – roots (eg carrots), bulbs (eg onions) leaves (eg spinach); it has examples of common and exotic vegetables.

A Day with Ling
by Ming Tsow (Hamish Hamilton)

Finger Foods
by Chris Deshpande (A&C Black)

Matza and Bitter Herbs
by Clive Lawston (Hamish Hamilton)

All these books are useful, simple information books about food from other countries and cultures. They can be used to support cooking and other activities relating to special festivals.

Recording and writing

Intended learning

For the children to write recipes, lists, charts, books; to look at environmental print - matching and recognising words in a context; to sequence instructions and to follow a sequence.

Introduction

Setting up a bird watching area gave the children many opportunities for writing in a context. It encouraged information and story writing, as well as spontaneous writing as a part of children's play.

Key vocabulary

bird cake, bird seed, bread, lard, melt, mix, pot

The activity

You will need:

For the hide – binoculars; bird books; clipboards, pencils and paper; bird identification charts, stories and information books about birds, a bird table or a bird feeder, bird seed, nuts, stale bread, raisins and lard for the bird cake, a saucepan and a large bowl, empty yoghurt and cream pots, and string, cards with instructions for making bird cake.

● Make a pictorial recipe for bird cake for the children to follow. It is made by breaking up stale bread and putting it in a bowl with some bird seed, nuts, raisins and melted lard. Mix everything together and spoon the mixture into yoghurt pots, pressing it down well. Tie a piece of string through a hole in the bottom of the pots, so they can be hung upside down on the bird table or from trees. Put them in a cool place for the bird cake to set, then help the children tie the pots from trees in the garden, for the birds to enjoy.

Bird watching encouraged the children to think about different ways of recording information.

● Set up a bird table or hanging bird feeder so that it is visible from a window in the nursery. Make a 'hide' – a bird watching area – by the window. You could make it look like a large bush by hanging leaves that have been painted or made from brown and green tissue paper.

● Stimulate the children's interest with stories, such as *The Lighthouse Keeper's Lunch* by Ronda and David Armitage (Hippo), about some hungry seagulls, and *Goodnight Owl* by Pat Hutchins. Talk about where birds live and what they eat. Use information books to identify common garden birds such as robins and blue tits.

● To prepare for using the hide, show the children an identification chart and encourage them to match the birds that come to the table with the ones in the pictures on the chart.

● Make signs saying BE QUIET and DON'T DISTURB THE BIRDS and put them up outside the hide. Have some signs in different languages and scripts. Parents might be willing to help if bilingual staff support isn't available.

● In the hide, the children can make a record of birds they see. Afterwards, they can make little books about the birds, referring to the identification chart.

Assessment and intervention

● Do the children choose to make lists, signs or charts in their play? Do they show any understanding of the conventions of these forms of writing?

● Can children talk about what they have written?

● Reading environmental print. Can children recognise some print from labels and packets, when they are put in a context? Can they match words on the instruction cards with print on labels?

● Can the children make a simple record of the number of birds they see at the bird table – either pictorial or symbolic? Can they read information from a simple chart?

● Can children put instruction cards in the correct sequence, or can they follow a sequence laid out by someone else?

Evidence of children's learning

We looked at cards, made previously by the teacher, which had instructions in words and pictures for making bird cake. The names of the ingredients had been cut out of packets and incorporated into the instruction cards. The children matched the words on the cards with the ingredients on the table. They recognised most of the ingredients. We talked about what we were going to do, and put the cards in the right order. Many of the children chose to write lists, books and charts in the bird hide.

Differentiating the activity

When recording the birds seen, some children could draw a picture of a number of birds. Others could draw a number of ticks on a chart.

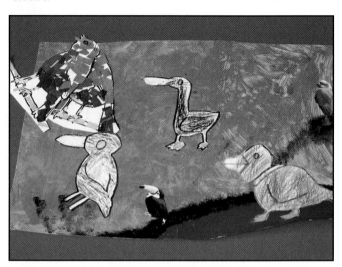

Some children might be able to talk about their writing in their books of birds. For others it might be appropriate to scribe their words, providing a model of a writer. While for others it might be enough to help them formulate their ideas in spoken language.

Some children might be able to use the initial letter of a word to give them a clue. They might use familiar logos to identify words. Point out initial sounds and talk about the names and sounds of some of the letters. Some children might be able to find letters that are in their own name.

If possible, give bilingual children the vocabulary for the ingredients for the bird cake in their mother tongue and in English. Ask parents to help, if you don't have bilingual staff.

Extension activities

● Carry on the bird watching activity over several days. Give children clipboards to take outside, to draw pictures and to do their own writing as they play.

● Plant some bird seed and see what happens!

● Stop everything for a few minutes and listen to the bird song.

● Have an investigation table with a bird's nest and possibly some eggshells. The children could try and build a nest from twigs, moss and leaves – and find out how clever birds are!

● Make a collage with egg shells, twigs, feathers and bird seed. Enjoy playing with the textures.

Working with parents

● Explain to parents that you are encouraging children to become bird watchers. Ask them to encourage their children to look out for birds at home and when they are out together.

● Have a recipe available for parents who might like to make bird cake at home.

● Ask the parents to encourage their children to draw pictures of birds that they can see from the window at home.

Other books to read

Goodnight Owl
by Pat Hutchins (Picture Puffin)

This introduces children to some common garden birds.

The Hunter and his Dog
by Brian Wildsmith (OUP)

This is a beautifully illustrated story about caring for birds.

Nine Ducks Nine
by Sarah Hayes (Walker)

This is a humorous story about how some ducks trick a fox which is trying to catch them. It is a good counting book.

But Where is the Green Parrot?
by Thomas and Wanda Zacharias (The Bodley Head)

This book has repeated phrases which children will join in with, and they enjoy finding the green parrot on each page.

Books featured in Starting to Read and Write

Phonics and key words

Who Sank the Boat? by Pamela Allen (Puffin)
The Gingerbread Man retold by Brenda Parkes and Judith Smith (Mimosa Publications)
The Runaway Chappatti by Ruth Creek (E J Arnold)
The Jolly Postman by Janet and Alan Ahlberg (Heinemann)
Wish You Were Here by Martina Selway (Red Fox)
Dear Zoo by Rod Campbell (Puffin)
Cops and Robbers by Janet and Alan Ahlberg (Fontana Picture Lions)
Where's My Teddy? by Jez Alborough (Walker Books)
This Is the Bear by Sarah Hayes (Walker Books)
Pass the Jam, Jim by Kate Umansky and Margaret Chamberlain (Red Fox)
The Very Hungry Caterpillar by Eric Carle (Puffin)
Handa's Surprise by Eileen Browne (Walker Books)
ABC Dinosaurs by Jan Pieńkowski (Heinemann)
Titch by Pat Hutchins (Picture Puffin)
The Tiny Seed by Eric Carle (Puffin)
Jaspar's Beanstalk by Nick Butterworth and Mick Inkpen (Hodder Children's Books)
Mouse Finds a Seed by Nicola Moon, illustrated by Anthony Morris (Pavilion)

Playing with stories

The Doorbell Rang by Pat Hutchins (Macmillan)
So Much by Trish Cooke, illustrated by Helen Oxenbury (Walker Books)
Ten In the Bed by Penny Dale (Walker Books)
The Giant Jam Sandwich by John Vernon Lord (Macmillan)
This is the Bear and the Picnic Lunch by Sarah Hayes and Helen Craig (Walker Books)
I Want My Dinner! by Tony Ross (Collins Picture Lions)
Once Upon a Time by John Prater (Walker Books)
The Sandwich that Max Made by Marcia Vaughan (Shortland Publications)
Hairy Tales and Nursery Crimes by Michael Rosen (Young Lions)
Jim and the Beanstalk by Raymond Briggs (Puffin)

The True Story of the Three Little Pigs by Jon Scieszka (Puffin)
Peace at Last by Jill Murphy (Macmillan)
Lullaby Hullabaloo by Mick Inkpen (Hodder and Stoughton)
Owl Babies by Martin Waddell (Walker)
The Litle Red Hen by Tony Bradman and Jenny Williams (Methuen)
Fantastic Mr Fox by Roald Dahl (Collins)
On the Way Home by Jill Murphy (Macmillan)
We're Going on a Bear Hunt by Michael Rosen and Helen Oxenbury (Walker Books)

Writing for a purpose

Pirate Poll by Susan Hill (Puffin)
Captain Abdul's Pirate School by Colin McNaughton (Walker Books)
Mudge the Smuggler by John Ryan (Macmillan)
Captain Pugwash stories by John Ryan (Puffin)
The Pirate and the Pig by Frank Rodgers (Puffin)
Captain Teachum's Buried Treasure by Korky Paul and Peter Carter (OUP)
Dear Zoo by Rod Campbell (Puffin)
A Message for Santa by Hiawyn Oram and Tony Ross (Andersen Press)
King Rollo's Letter and Other Stories by David McKee (Beaver Books)
Mr Gumpy's Outing by John Burningham (Puffin)
Teddybears Take the Train by Susanna Gretz and Alison Sage (Hippo books)
Are We Nearly There? Louis Baum (Magnet)
Stone Soup by Tony Ross (Beaver Books)
Stir Fry by Ruth Nagrath Woodbridge (A&C Black)
A Day with Ling by Ming Tsow (Hamish Hamilton)
Finger Foods by Chris Deshpande (A&C Black)
Matza and Bitter Herbs by Clive Lawston (Hamish Hamilton)
Goodnight Owl by Pat Hutchins (Picture Puffin)
The Hunter and his Dog by Brian Wildsmith (OUP)
Nine Ducks Nine by Sarah Hayes (Walker)
But Where is the Green Parrot? by Thomas and Wanda Zacharias (The Bodley Head)

First published 1998 by A & C Black (Publishers) Ltd, 35 Bedford Row, London WC1R 4JH
Text copyright © Julie Cigman 1998. Illustrations copyright © Alison Dexter 1998.
Photographs by John Brennan pp 13, 21, 25, 33, 41, 45, 49 and Matthew Cannon pp 18, 29, 31, 53, 57, 61.
Cover photograph by Alex Brattell. The author and publisher would like to thank Alison Street, the staff and children at Bartlemas Nursery School, Rose Hill First School nursery class and Appley-Dappley's Day Nursey.

ISBN 0-7136-4856-2
A CIP catalogue record for this book is available from the British Library.

Printed in China through Colorcraft Ltd.